BODYWORKS

eyes

Katherine Goode

BLACKBIRCH PRESS, INC.

WOODBRIDGE, CONNECTICUT

Published by Blackbirch Press, Inc.
260 Amity Road
Woodbridge, CT 06525

e-mail: staff@blackbirch.com
web site: www.blackbirch.com

Printed in Hong Kong

First published 1999 by
MACMILLAN EDUCATION AUSTRALIA PTY LTD
627 Chapel Street, South Yarra 3141

10 9 8 7 6 5 4 3 2 1

Photo Credits:
Cover photo: ©PhotoDisc
Page 1: International Photo Library; pages 11, 20: A.N.T.; pages 12a, 12b:
AUSCAPE/©Sarah Wing; page 14: AUSCAPE/©Jean-Paul Ferrero; page 27: Coo-ee
Picture Library; p. 18: Graham Meadows; pages 4, 5, 21, 29, 30: Great Southern Stock;
pages 6, 7, 9, 13, 19, 23, 24, 25, 26, 28: The Picture Source.

Library of Congress Cataloging-in-Publication Data
Goode, Katherine, 1949–
Eyes / by Katherine Goode.
        p.   cm. — (Bodyworks)
    Includes index.
    Summary: Explains the functions of the different parts of the eye.
    ISBN 1-56711-495-4 (hardcover : alk. paper)
    1. Eye—Juvenile literature. [1. Eye.] I. Title.
QP475.7.G66   2000
612.8'4—dc21
                                                                    00-008105
                                                                    CIP

Contents

4   The eyes

6   Protecting the eyes

8   Parts of the eye

16   How you see

18   Tears

20   Animal eyes

22   Sight problems

26   Blindness

28   Glasses and contact lenses

29   Eye care

31   Glossary

32   Index

The eyes

You see the world through your eyes. Eyes let you see color, movement, size, and shape.

You use your eyes for almost everything you do. You use them to read, write, play games, and watch television.

Protecting the eyes

Your eye is a soft, delicate organ. It is protected by your eyelids, eyelashes, and eye socket.

Your eyelids are made up of fatty **tissues**. These tissues can close quickly to protect your eyes from flying objects or bright light.

eyelid

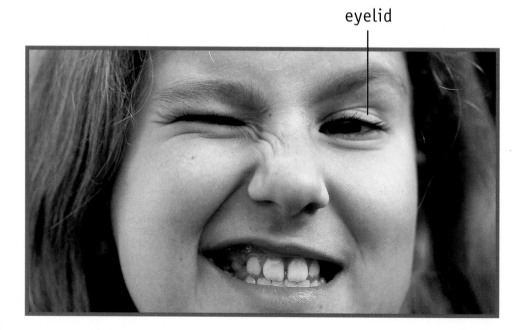

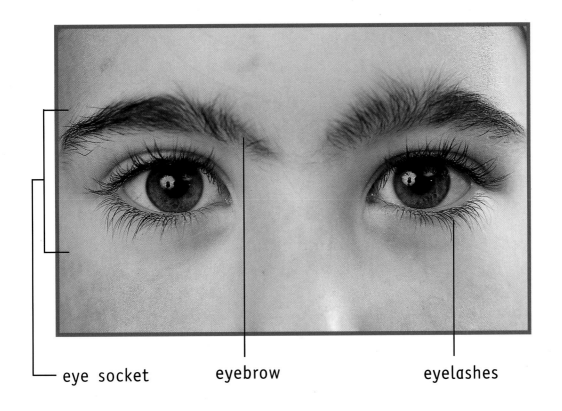

eye socket   eyebrow   eyelashes

Eyelashes grow on the edge of your eyelids. They are a row of short hairs. When your eyelids are partly closed, eyelashes can screen out dust and insects.

Your bony eye socket is part of your skull. It surrounds and protects your eye.

Parts of the eye

Your eyeball is round. It has a small bulge at the front. This is the part you see when you are looking at someone's eyes.

Your eye is divided into 3 layers. There is an outer layer, a middle layer, and an inner layer.

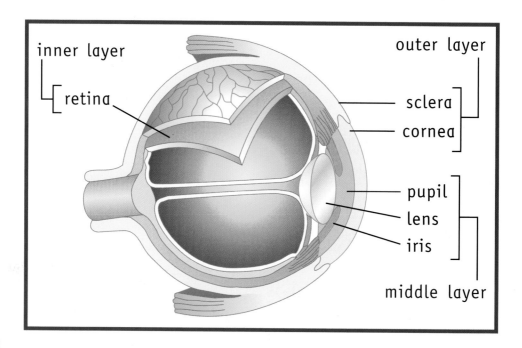

Outer layer

The sclera and cornea make up the outer layer. They are made up of tough tissues that protect your eye. The sclera is the white part of your eye. The cornea is the **transparent** part at the front of your eye, which lets in light.

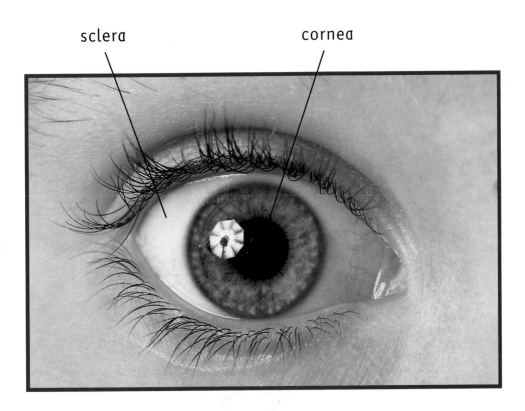

sclera   cornea

Middle layer

The middle layer contains the iris, pupil, and lens. The iris is the colored part of your eye. At the center of the iris is an opening called the pupil. The pupil controls the amount of light that enters your eye. The lens is transparent. Light goes through the lens to the back of your eye.

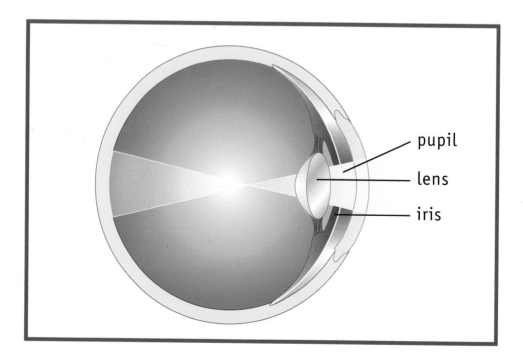

pupil

lens

iris

An albino
owl has no
melanin so
its eyes are
pink.

Melanin is a dark **pigment** that is found in the
iris. Brown eyes have more melanin in the iris,
and blue eyes have less melanin.

Some people and animals have no melanin.
Their irises are pink. They are called albinos.

Your pupil changes size according to the amount of light that enters your eye.

In dim light, your pupil becomes bigger to let in more light.

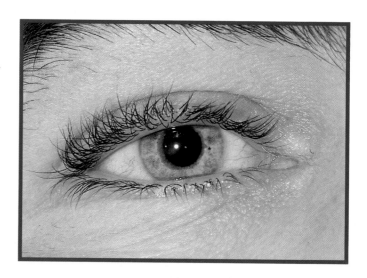

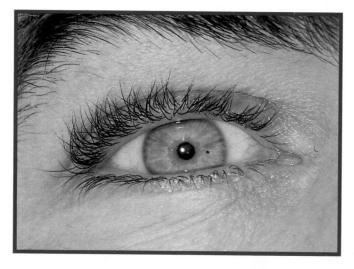

In bright light, your pupil becomes smaller to reduce the amount of light that enters your eye.

Your lens changes shape to bring an object into focus. When you look at an object that is far away, the muscle around your lens relaxes and flattens it. When you look at an object that is nearby, the muscle tightens and makes your lens rounder and thicker.

The lens in your eye works like the lens in a camera. It cannot focus on a nearby object and a distant one at the same time.

Inner layer

The inner layer of your eye is called the retina. It contains millions of cells called rods and cones. The rods allow you to see different shades of gray and to see in dim light. The cones allow you to see colors and to see in bright light.

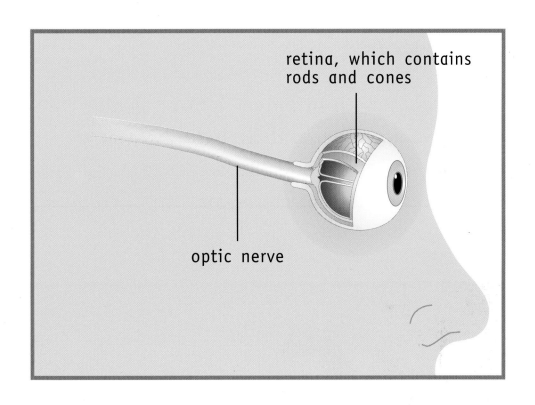

retina, which contains rods and cones

optic nerve

Nerve fibers are attached to the rods and cones. They join together in the middle of the retina to form the optic nerve. The rods and cones change light rays into electrical signals. These signals are sent through the optic nerve to your brain. Your brain changes the signals into pictures.

How you see

Your eyes can see in bright light or shadow, but they cannot see when there is no light at all. Each of your eyes works like a camera. Light rays reflected from an object and pass through your lens. The lens focuses the light on the retina.

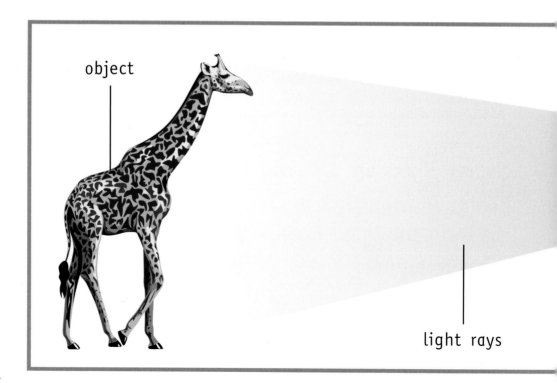

object

light rays

Nerve impulses are sent to your brain through the optic nerve. Although the message is sent upside down, your brain is able to recognize that the image is really right side up. When you see a giraffe, for example, your optic nerve sends the image upside down, but your brain knows the giraffe is really right side up.

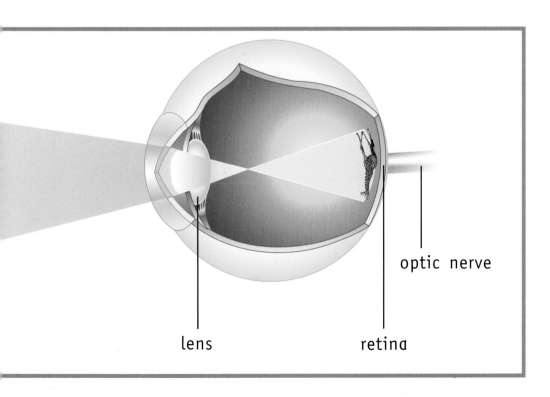

lens

optic nerve

retina

Tears

Tears stop your eyes from drying up. They also help fight **bacteria**. Blinking helps spread the tear fluid over your eyes.

Tears overflow when you cry.

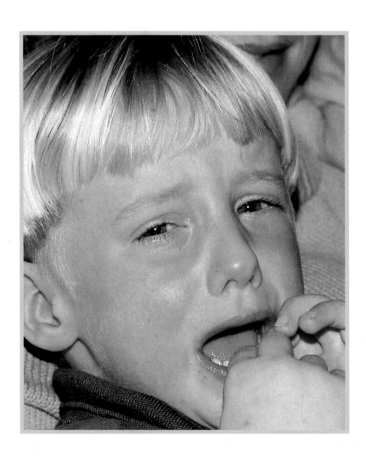

When you cry, tears drain through a **tear duct** into your nose. That's why you often need to blow your nose after you cry.

Animal eyes

The eyes of **nocturnal** animals, such as cats and rats, only have rod cells. Animals that hunt at night have large eyes and pupils that help them to see better in dim light.

The eye of a dolphin has 7,000 times more rod cells than a human eye. This allows a dolphin to see in deep water, where there is little light.

Sight problems

Many people have problems seeing. The most common eye problems are nearsightedness and farsightedness. People who are nearsighted cannot focus clearly on objects that are far away. People who are farsighted have trouble seeing objects that are close-up.

People who are farsighted need glasses to help them read.

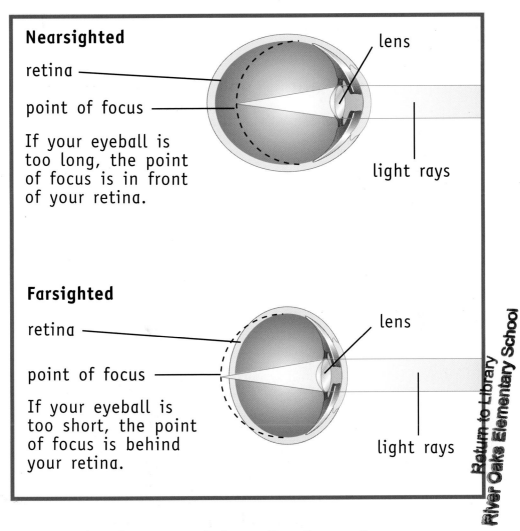

Nearsighted

retina

lens

point of focus

If your eyeball is too long, the point of focus is in front of your retina.

light rays

Farsighted

retina

lens

point of focus

If your eyeball is too short, the point of focus is behind your retina.

light rays

Nearsightedness and farsightedness happen when the shape of your eyeballs is either too wide or too narrow.

Some people are color blind. They cannot tell the difference between some colors. In a few cases, they may not be able to see any colors at all. These people see only shades of gray.

Some people who are color blind cannot tell the difference between red and green.

Eye problems can be present at birth, or they can develop at any time. An optometrist checks your eyes for vision problems. If you have eye problems, you may need to see a doctor called an ophthalmologist.

Blindness

Some people are blind, which means they cannot see anything. A person may be born blind or may lose sight later in life. Some people are partly blind. Special glasses with tiny computers may help some blind people to see again.

Blind people can use guide dogs to help them.

There are many special services for blind people, such as guide dogs and books on tape. Many blind people have also learned to read in Braille. Braille is a writing system that uses raised dots on a page. To read, a person feels the dots with his or her fingers.

Glasses and contact lenses

Glasses have lenses set in frames. They are worn in front of your eyes. Contact lenses are thin lenses that sit directly on the surface of your cornea. Both kinds of lenses help your eyes to see more clearly. Today, laser surgery can correct some vision problems.

Eye care

The most common injuries to the eye are caused by being struck, or by dirt or small particles that enter the eye. Most particles can be removed by flooding the eye with water.

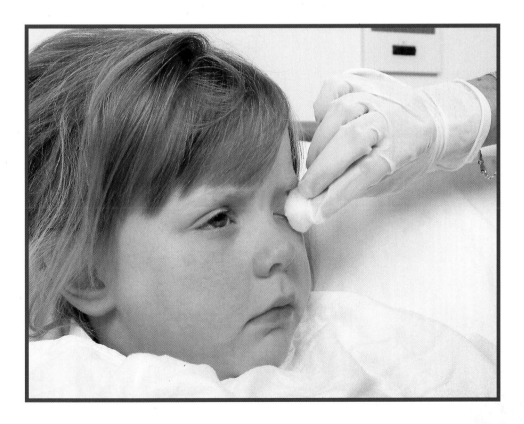

Your eyes should always be protected when you play a sport. A helmet with a face mask can be worn during hockey, baseball, or football. Special goggles are sometimes worn in sports such as basketball, tennis, or swimming.

Glossary

bacteria   germs

nocturnal   awake and active mainly at night

pigment   the material found in skin, hair, and eyes which gives them color

tear duct   short tube in the lower eyelid that drains tears away into the nose

tissues   the matter that living things are made of

transparent   materials that light can pass through

Index

albino 11

blindness 26-27
Braille 27

color blindness 24
cones 14-15
contact lenses 28

farsightedness 22-23

iris 10-11

laser surgery 28
lens 10, 13, 16-17

nearsightedness 22-23
nocturnal animals 20

optic nerve 15
opthalmologist 25
optometrist 25

pupil 10, 12, 20

retina 14-15, 16-17
rods 14-15, 20

sclera 9

tears 18-19